THE POWER OF **VISION** WITH A

PURPOSE

MARCUS LISBOA

The power of vision with a purpose
How the Power of Vision and Disruptive Technologies can transform and impact
your life and the world

1st Edition
Marcus Lisboa, 2020

Edition, revision:
Suellen de Araujo Costa

Cover:
Jonatas Santos

Layout and Graphic Design:
Marcus V. P. Alcântara

Editorial Coordination:
Nilce Sousa

English Edition:
Bianca E. Menezes Alves

Published in Brazil by: **Cevi Produções**
CNPJ 07.856.521/0001-94
Caldas Novas, Goiás - Brasil
Instagram: **@editoracevi**
ceviproducoes@gmail.com

L769p Lisboa, Marcus
    The power of vision with a purpose / Marcus Lisboa; coordination
Nilce Sousa; English Edition: Bianca E. Menezes Alves. -
    1. ed. - Caldas Novas-GO: CEVI, 2020.
    54p. ; 21 cm.

    Inclui bibliografia
    ISBN: 978-65-5642-034-9

1. Leadership - Religious aspects. 2. Creativity. 3. Psychology
Religious. 4. Disruptive technologies. 5. Self-knowledge. I. Title.

CDU: 658.012.4

Catalogação na publicação por: Onélia Silva Guimarães CRB-14/071

This is the third book in a series composed of three titles: "Cryptocurrencies: The Money of the Future", "The Four Types of Transformative Intelligence: Intelligences Applied to Christian Transformation in the Digital Age" and "The Power of Vision with a Purpose: How Disruptive Technologies can transform and impact your life and the world."

The sequence entitled "Digital Economic Series" seeks to explain complex themes, such as disruptive technologies, the new financial model brought by the emergence of virtual currencies, and especially, to show you how we can connect to these issues so present nowadays, to experience the breadth of its benefits, managing its use and serving the purpose and vision intended for us.

My wish is that you open yourself up to discover this relevant content, and allow yourself to have a new vision about the economy and its role within it, becoming a transforming agent in the environment where you live.

ACKNOWLEDGMENTS

My especial thanks to Paula Vaz, Robson Silva, Marselha Samora, Harlisson Charley, Alexandre Hilgert and Alexandre Salgado, Carlos Guerreiro, Fabio Reis, Rubens Lemos, Romulo Souto, Pastor Carlos Almeida, Pastor Meire, Pastor Sidnei Borges, Pastor Eliane Pereira, Pastor Jean Kleber, Pastor Glabson, Pastor Joseph Maluta, Bishop JB Carvalho, Bishop Dirce Carvalho and Thomas Carter.

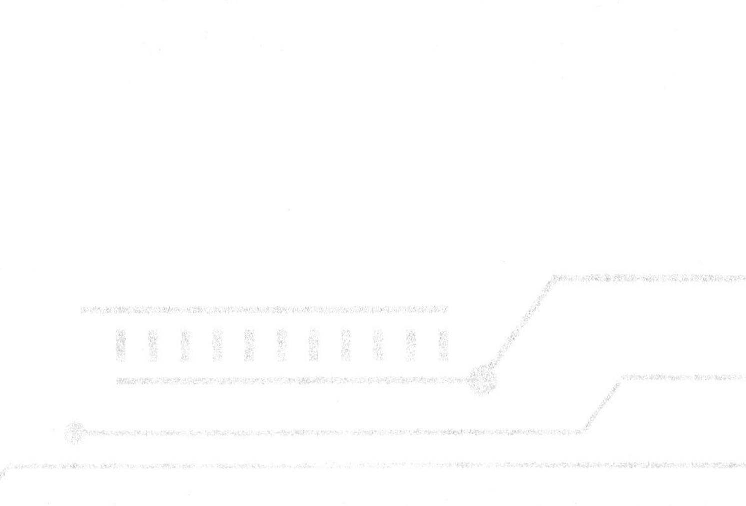

DEDICATION

I dedicate this book to my parents *(in Memorium)* Alfredo Almeida and Irene Lisboa, to my brothers Sérgio Luis, Carlos Alberto, Paulo César and Luis Cláudio, to my children Marcus Jr., Debora Regina, Jessyca Cristina, Priscila Maria, Andressa Santos, and Vinicius Galvão, to my beloved wife and companion Silvania Cristina Viegas, to my stepchildren, Junior, Moacir Neto, and Silveria Viegas, to my brothers-in-law, sisters-in-law, grandchildren and to all my nephews and friends.

ABOUT THE AUTHOR

Marcus Lisboa, Systems and O&M Analyst, Cryptographer, Specialist in Public Interest Politics and Public Politics and Government Manager, Specialist in Disruptive Technologies, with International Certification in Digital Transformation & Blockchain, Founder of the Eco-System and Proof of Consensus called Proof of Participation – PoP (Blockchain Permitted), Blockchain enthusiast based on Proof of Consensus – PoC – Proof of Capacity, author of the following titles: Cryptocurrencies – The Money of the Future; The Power of Vision with a Purpose, and The Four Types of Transformative Intelligences. Founding President of the National Institute of Public

Politics Excellence – INEPP, Editor-in-Chief of the WikiCryptoMarket.com Blog, Creator of the Public Interest – IP Channel, and member of the Council of Presidents of the Christian Center for Public Life – CCPL, known in Brazil as Conservative Christian Organization, with headquarters in Washington and national headquarters in Brasília – Distrito Federal, and creator of the professional education portal in the area of Crypto Assets, Crypto Trader and Crypto-Economy www.cryptotech.com.br.

Summary

INTRODUCTION

We are daily exposed to the new, facing a world that demands constant transformation from us, and that is why we need to keep in mind who and what we are following. This concerns who we want to be and where we want to go, the vision that moves us, and in which we move.

This book talks about the power of vision, the ability it gives us to pursue and persist in an ideal that benefits not only ourselves, but the whole that is around us.

I believe that this year marks the beginning of a new decade of transformation and overcoming, and only those who are willing to change and pursue God's vision for their lives will succeed.

For this reason, I want to invite you to immerse yourself in the vision and understand the power that emanates from it to move from a mediocre and unsuccessful life to an extraordinary experience and existence.

CHAPTER 1

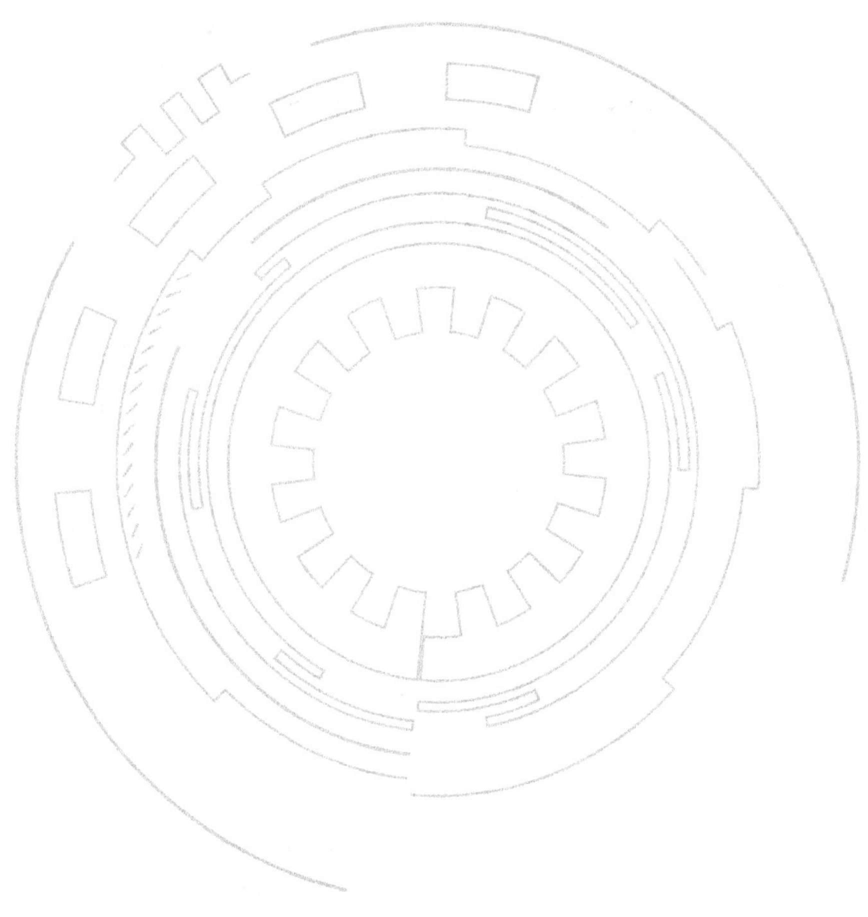

First of all, I would like to clarify that, at birth, we received from God two types of visions: the first would be the physical or natural vision, and the second the spiritual or supernatural vision. Physical vision is the ability to see what is around us, such as contemplating nature or the wonders of the Creator.

Spiritual vision, on the other hand, is the ability to see beyond the physical, much broader, more powerful, and transformative. It is also gifted to us at birth, but not in the one that lasts approximately nine months, where the structure that will enable natural vision is formed. The spiritual vision is a gift given to the newborn; those who gave their lives to the complete lordship of God, and from then on, were born spiritually.

In this new birth, our spiritual eyes are opened. Unfortunately, there are Christians who have experienced the new birth; however, they still have limited vision or are completely blind, which is a huge spiritual and natural loss, since spiritual failure results in little natural willingness.

However, this book is an invitation to those who desire this transformative vision, which will enable them to see far beyond the limitations common to us human beings and will elevate us to a place of greatness and fulfillment. It is like a breath of life for those who may be discouraged, with no prospect of the future, especially at the moment we are facing, so that they can have their vision restored and their eyes open to the new that is before us, so we can make a difference in a society fallen and lacking references.

VISION
RESTORATION

Jesus was and remains as the most exceptional doctor in the universe. He cured everything from skin diseases to bone structure diseases. But as I walk through the Gospels, I realize how much He dedicated himself to curing diseases related to vision. He was an expert in physical vision, but even more in spiritual vision.

God cares about what we see because what we see spiritually will determine how far we will go, whether we will succeed or fail. You can't reach a goal without knowing what the vision and motivation would be.

We see in various biblical passages how God restored people's vision. In Mark 8, we understand that Jesus left with the disciples for the city of Bethsaida, and there He met a blind man. At that moment, Jesus reached out his hand, took him out of the village, and healed him.

In Genesis 15:5, God asks Abraham to raise his eyes and contemplate the stars in the sky, determining that his offspring would be like that, countless, beyond what he could imagine and see with physical eyes.

Another relevant event was when Jesus, after spitting in His hands, places them over the eyes of the blind man. He asks the blind man what he was seeing. Soon, the man replies that he saw "men like trees that walk," which leads us to conclude that that blind man had already seen, that is, he was not born without vision, but at that moment, he needed the healing touch of the Lord.

These are all examples of restored vision, and I can guarantee that if we don't have our vision restored, we'll stop yielding and will retreat. Over time, the passion for serving the work is lost, religiosity takes over, and the dreams and original vision of God wane to the point of turning away entirely from Him.

But if you are reading this book today, it is because God does not want you blind spiritually, aimlessly and out of your path, and living below what He planned for your life. So today, I invite you to surrender to Him and let Him touch your vision, as He has done with everyone who has approached Him for help.

CHAPTER 3

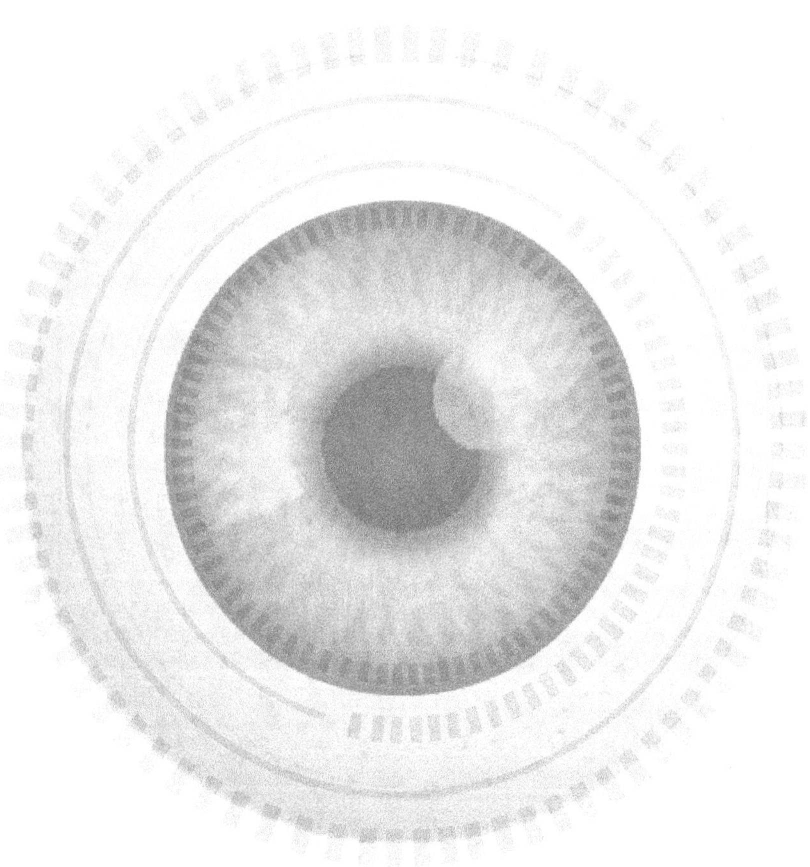

Here, I would like to propose an analogy that I consider to be important about the physical vision that is totally related to spiritual vision. As I said initially, we are dichotomous beings, and we have both natural and spiritual vision. So, if we protect and value physical vision, there is no reason to act less carefully with spiritual vision.

Experienced researchers have found that a disease that affects man's vision, known as Usher Syndrome, develops when someone stays for a long time, without living or having contact with other people, without being able to hear the voice of other human beings. It is blindness associated with deafness.

Something of this nature brings profound teaching because when there is no communion, there is degeneration. We can extend this to communion with other "visionary" people, and also with God because of the lack of constant communication with Him is the source of incalculable damage.

The Bible tells us that "faith comes by hearing the Word of God," and those who do not hear it lose their sight, their direction, and their sense of purpose. And the person who moves away from communion with other people, who share the same values and the same goals, also loses his sight.

In this sense, I place discipleship as an essential tool to develop the vision; it is crucial to have someone to accompany, advise, and encourage us in times of crisis. This broadens the vision, produces focus, and strengthens the goals, in addition to enabling an essential healing tool: confession.

The Bible also tells us that when "we confess our sins to one another, we are healed." When a relationship of trust and communion is established, and we can speak freely of what torments us, our vision receives a powerful remedy, and we can see healthily again.

VISIONARY
LEADERSHIP

I am sure that the most important characteristic of a leader's life is vision. The ability to see the present and move towards a future, which for others may be totally obscure, but for him, it is as clear as water, a goal for which it is worth paying the necessary price.

But, unfortunately, many men and women choose to remain blurred. Instead of seeing people, they see trees. The tree represents the physical, the materialism. We need to see people because God calls us to see people (John 3:16). Jesus saw everyone and taught them to behold the Lord.

Some leaders do not achieve their goals because they have a very limited vision. We must flee from places and circumstances where everything is limited to what is merely material. In Revelation 3:18, God's message to the Laodicea Church was to "anoint your eyes" to be able to see. The vision of that people needed to be restored.

This is because our vision is not always aligned with that of God. We fail to realize what really has value, and that is why we "stumble" like a blind man facing a rocky path, or even fail to understand the actual reality that surrounds us.

In II Kings 6:14, we have an example of someone who did not see with the eyes of God and had to have his vision restored by the Lord. Gehazi, a servant of the man of God, had been terrified by the sight of the troop of horses and chariots surrounding the city, but the prophet Elisha prayed and asked the Lord to open his eyes to what was really there (II Kings 14:17).

The Bible tells us that the man's eyes were so opened that he could then see that an army with horses and chariots surrounded them. Similar to the servant, some are terrified of problems, and fail to see that there is an army of God to help us, and win any battle.

As in the past, many leaders today do not achieve victory because they can only visualize conflict. Their vision is stagnant in traumas, unsuccessful experiences, in failure, and in their genetic and behavioral heritage.

That is why I have proposed empowerment and knowledge as real keys to change. You cannot change a route without self-knowledge and identification of your own natural and developed talents, and especially, you cannot follow a vision without prior knowledge of where you are and where you want to go.

This book is not called "The Power of Vision with a Purpose" for nothing; after all, the vision has power and purpose. Power is the ability to aggregate people around the same goal and accomplish it, and the purpose is the reason why we do what we do.

I will talk about these two aspects in more detail later, but it is worth saying that the vision that can actually produce something is linked to the spiritual. It is a fusion between physical and supernatural vision.

Thus, armed with the power of vision, we can not only fulfill but encourage others to get there as well. So that, if someone approaches you and emphatically says that they are going to change the world, there must be agreement on your part, so that the world can be restored to fundamental and essential points, by visionary and accomplished leaders.

> *"Where there is no revelation,*
> *the people cast off restraint; but*
> *blessed is he who keeps the law."*
>
> Proverbs 29:18

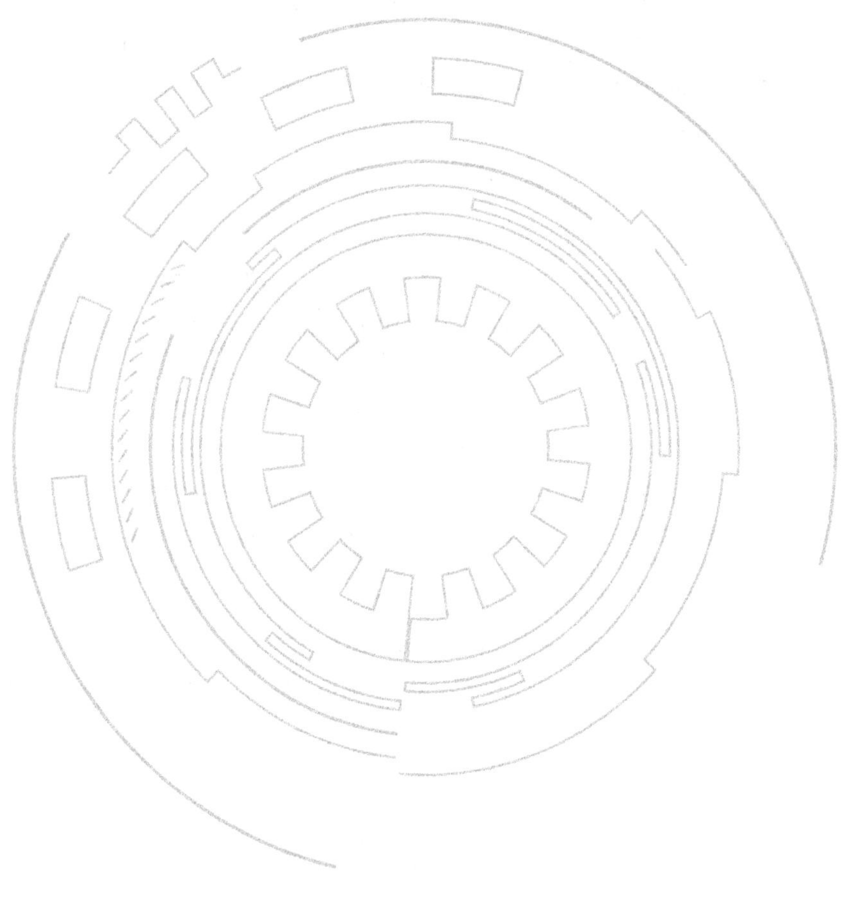

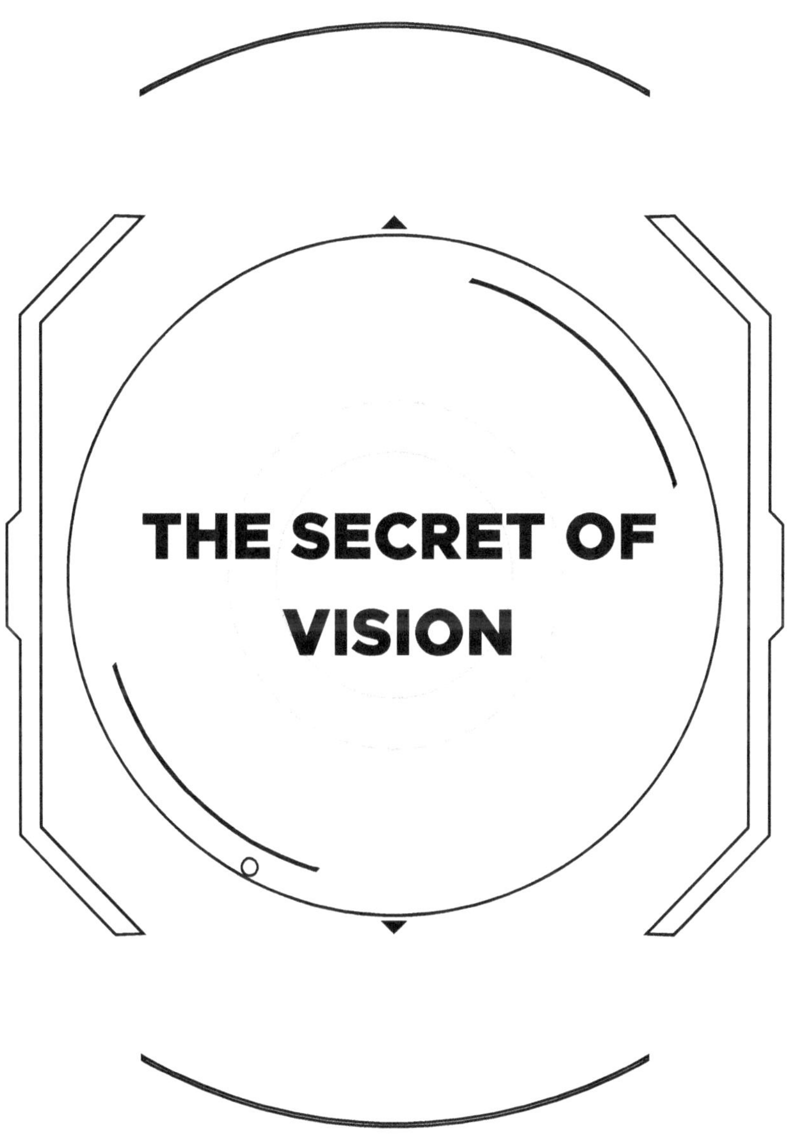

THE SECRET OF
VISION

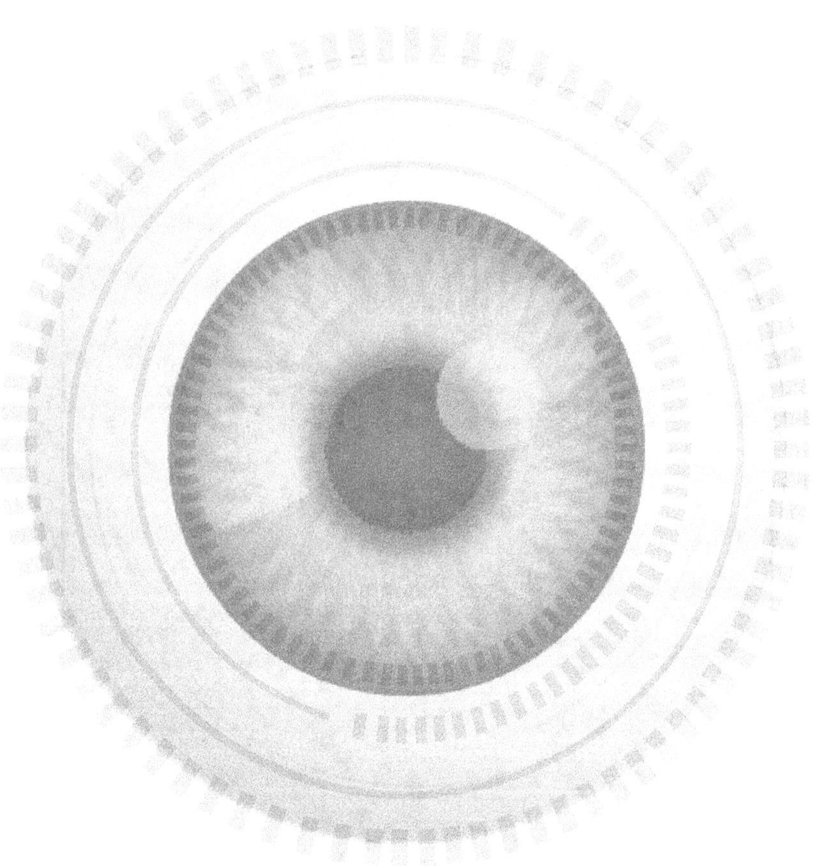

We have already said that the vision that should guide our achievements must be primarily spiritual, that is, provided by God. I dare say that it is nothing more than a painting containing a photograph engraved on your heart, capable of making you follow it all the time and at any cost. Thus, the permanent vision will always speak louder than your problem, which is momentary.

Also, spiritual vision can be obtained through the following channels:

1 – From the dream – Example: The revelation to Joseph of Egypt, who through two dreams, understood his mission and purpose of life, and remained in it even in the face of the worst circumstances.

2 – From the Word through prayer – Example: While praying to God, a word appears in your heart, and it will guide you,

restore you, and position you concerning the truth that has been already placed within you.

3 – Association by model – Example: it is a way for God to generate in you the vision that you have of the person next to me. This can determine what God may be putting in your heart. Another example is: If I walk with a man of God, it will be a blessing, and will open the door for me to grow in the spiritual world. (Lion walks with Lion, Cat walks with Cat).

I would like to emphasize this last point by recalling the story of Elijah and Elisha. They were so close and connected that, when Elijah was about to ascend to Heaven, Elisha asked for the double anointing for himself. This is something very impressive because Elijah was not just anybody, but a man who operated incredibly, and so it was with Elisha too. The association has this power to transfer vision and grant power to carry it out.

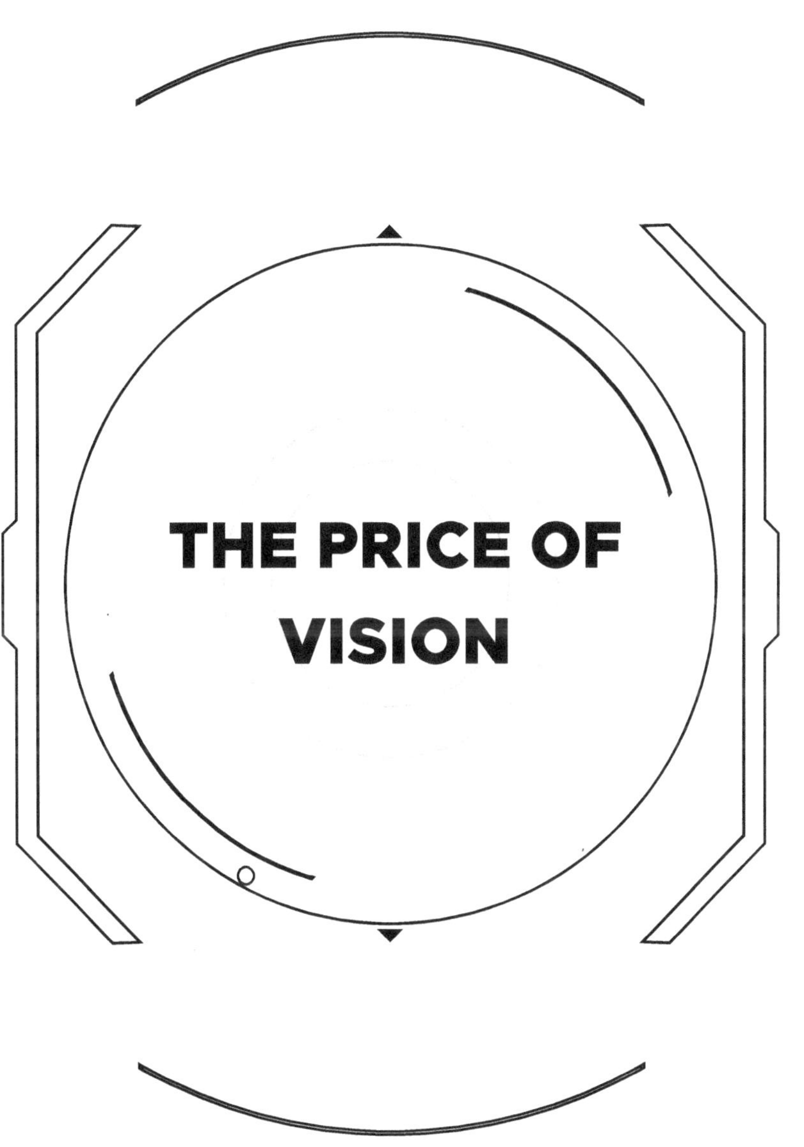
THE PRICE OF
VISION

ike everything that is really important, the vision has a price. To reach and embrace God's vision, you need:

Faith

God will always ask you for something that you don't think you can do and may not seem to have the resources to do it, but when you put your faith in action and believe that the one who called is the one who enables you, you can launch yourself and pass from one simple dreamer to a conqueror.

Patience

Patience is the quality of those who wait in peace because they trust in the God who serves and know of his supernatural power. Abraham is a very faithful example of this. God promised him a son. However, his first attempt was the result of his impatience, and only 25 years later, the son of the promise arrived, even with his wife's disbelief.

Achieving also requires patience, the vision that God gave you always stands the test of time, and only those who wait patiently achieve it. Patience has nothing to do with apathy; it is much more linked to a vigorous and mature faith.

Initiative

The initiative is the hallmark of the man and woman of vision. When God feeds a dream within him, he is motivated and takes the appropriate initiative to leverage that dream.

Perspective

Perspective has to do with the ability to see far, to believe in something even if that is not yet a doable reality. In 1774, John Adams announced the vision of a new nation, with a union of 13 states, independent of parliament and the reign of England. And it happened. In less than two years, the United States of America was born.

At the end of the 18th century, two brothers, Wilbur and Orville Wright heralded the era of flying machines. After 13 years of various experiences, it happened. The age of air travel had begun.

William Wilberforce gave the summons in the English parliament saying that men, women, and children, would no longer be bought, and slavery should be abolished. Four days before his death, 18 years later, his bill was passed.

I could mention many other situations in which people had perspective and thought ahead of their time. Still, the most important thing is to know that this quality is essential to get us where we want to go, and gives us the power to see and be part of the break and the evolution of this new digital economy.

Purpose

I believe that it is not enough to be innovative; it is necessary to have a purpose. I also believe that the vision that remains is one that has a perennial motivation, and that seeks to influence people beyond our own niche positively.

I have had the perception that we have been in the last few days, and a new cloak will fall on some of the true Christian Leaders, the "Spiritual Parents of multitudes, to share with all Spiritual children" and reach the People of God, seeking to generate a broad spiritual vision, accepting, promoting and causing a break with a transformative vision and, in particular, experience a real disruption of a new Collaborative and 100% Digital and secure Economy that is known as Crypto-Economy.

And all of this with a very clear and defined purpose: profound changes in digital finance, allowing us to carry out ministerial service, with the generation and distribution of new wealth in favor of the Kingdom of God in the first place. And the Bible is emphatic in saying that, to those who seek the Kingdom first, all other things are added.

We are facing a big break of paradigms, causing significant transformations, empowering people, generating and distributing wealth in a decentralized, safe, and socially and humanely way, where the relationships and financial transactions will be increasingly digital and personal, through the use of Peer to Peer platforms (person to person) increasingly driven in this new digital economy.

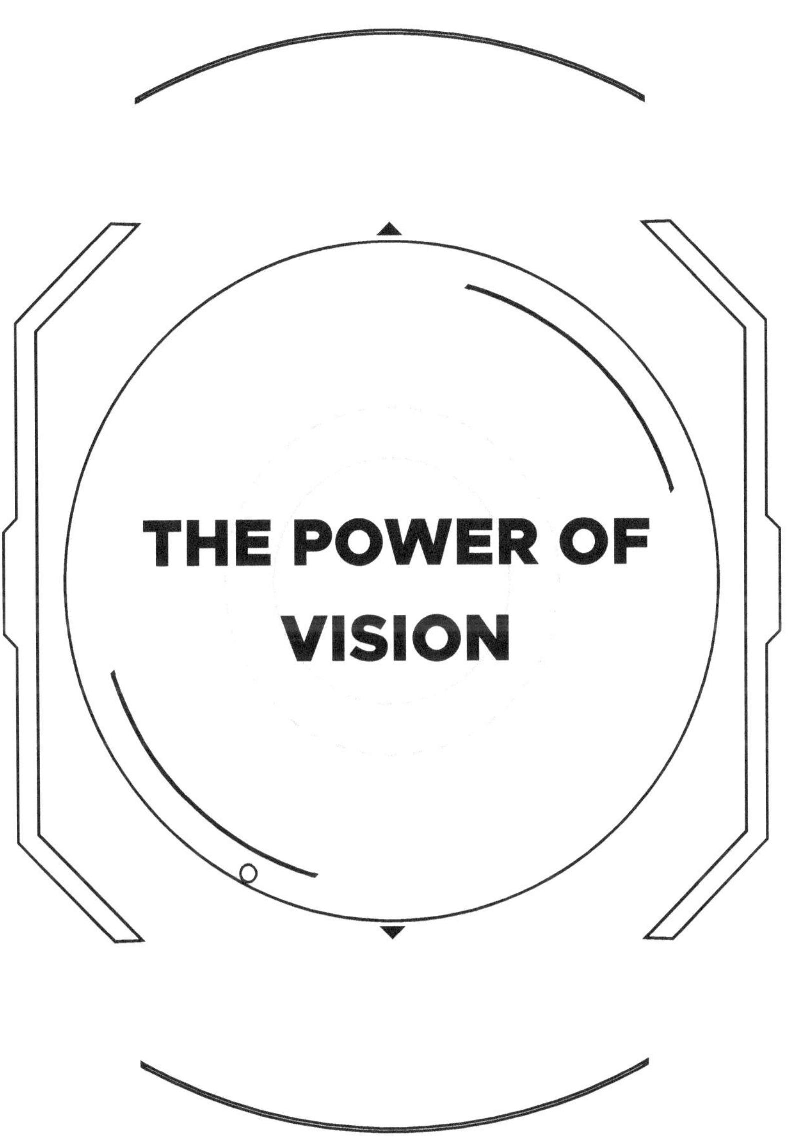
THE POWER OF
VISION

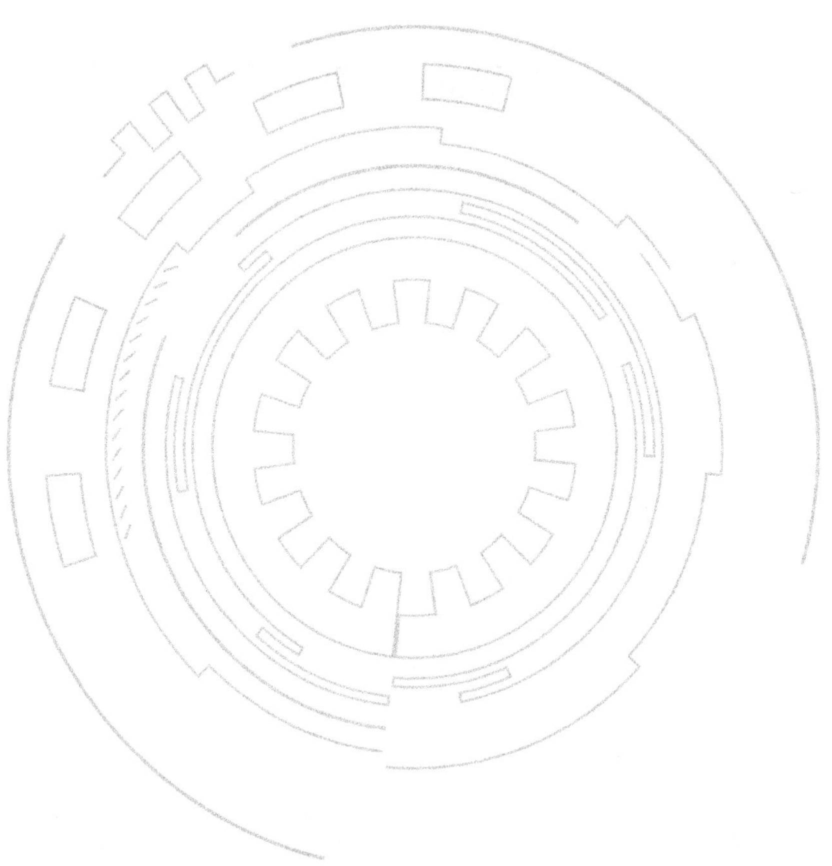

What about the power of vision? What would it be? We are talking about the most powerful weapon for the transformation of the world. I ask you, what do disruptive people have in common? It is an irresistible ideal. What makes us understand that visualizing and persisting is the essence of a true leader.

Subtract the ability to visualize his ideal from a great leader, and he will die. Vision is the fuel that keeps the leader moving forward. It is the energy that creates the action. It is the clear call that raises the flame. Without vision, we lose the vitality that makes us keep our dreams and ideals alive.

The power of vision with a purpose of benefiting the kingdom is all that, applied to the spiritual universe, since vision, power, leadership, and authority, in whatever it may be, is granted by God. From that, strategies are created, tools, methodologies, technologies, and processes for its perfect implementation, seeking the Kingdom of God in the first place so that all other things can be added.

Human evolution is incredible, and at the same time strange, because every time we encounter the new, we have a feeling that does not concern us, that we are mere spectators in the face of these incredible transformations. However, the only certainty we have is that, to live in this new world that is emerging, it will be necessary to make a radical change.

Change involves our attitudes, thoughts, and demands great transformation from us, we have to transform limitations into boldness, dreams into actions, defeat in victories, difficulties in opportunities, tears in smiles, longings in joys, doubts in certainties, fear in courage, and even hate in love.

Suddenly, the student will have to become a researcher; our eyes will have to learn to see the world differently; rather than seeing the changes, we need to feel them with the soul and the heart, far above our own reason.

All of this has a great name: the Power of Vision, the power to dream of what does not exist, the ability to create something that nobody has ever thought of before, the power to get where only our thoughts have dared to go, and it is this thought that everyone has to discover within himself.

CHAPTER 8

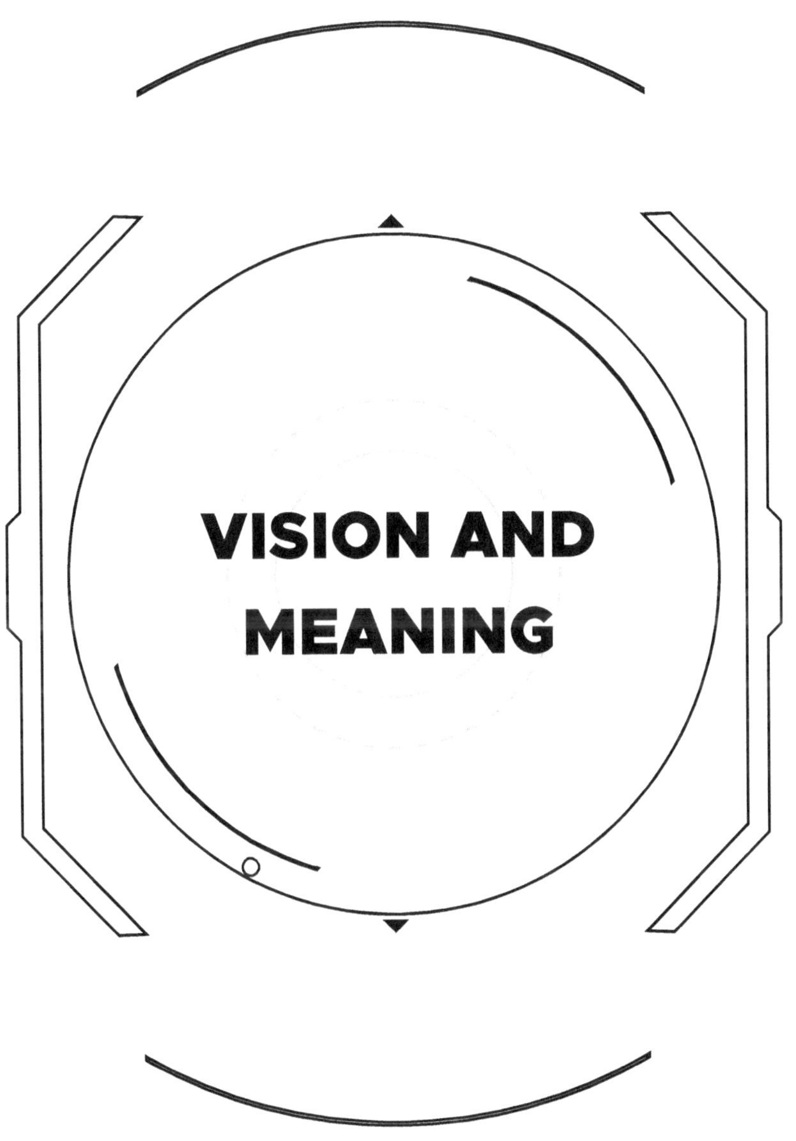

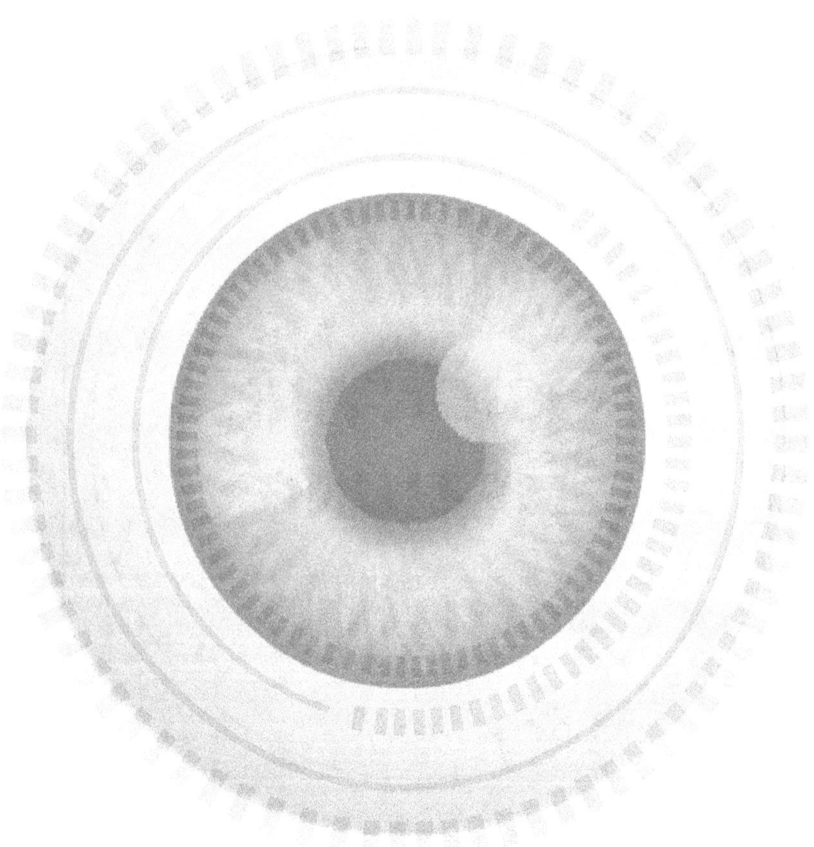

ime can be a great executioner because every day, it is necessary to shorten it to do things, to learn, to develop, and live intensely. Have you realized that we often fail to understand the real meaning of our existence?

It is amazing how this crazy rush in the modern world has blindfolded our eyes, to observe and understand the simplest things, and it is in these things so simple that the essence of the universe is hidden.

It is in a child's free imagination that fantasies become realities; it is in the light wings of birds that the secret of flying is kept; it is in the fragility of flowers that is the perfume and beauty that sweetens our spirit; it is in the richness of the earth that seeds are transformed into fruits; it is in the invisible waves of the satellite that a new way of communicating in a universal language emerges.

It is also in the dark and frantic creaking of cars and airplanes, that distances are shortened; it is in the magic keys of computers and in the fastest chips, that an incredible world of virtual elements appears; and it is mainly, in the passion for life that is reborn the certainty of a new tomorrow.

Man has already surpassed his limits and has reached the stars and is increasingly heading towards the unknown "world." Each one of us is a universe to be unveiled, each one of us brings wisdom within us, and only the skillful hands of a God were able to heal.

Therefore, we must learn to use this force, often asleep within our hearts and minds. We must stop for a moment, look carefully around us and inside ourselves and ask: what have I really done to be better? What have I done to make a difference? How have I viewed my plans and goals? Have I been only a mere spectator of my life?

CONCLUSION

The power of vision is nothing more than the ability to dream, it is the joy of living, it is the desire to learn, it is the patience and the affection to teach, it is the ability to understand human failures, and especially, the sincere feeling of friendship, respect, and love for your fellow man.

This world, in which we live, has several phases, various tastes, various creeds, many customs, multiple religions. Still, love remains one, a unique feeling that resists through wars, injustices, despite the selfishness and hypocrisy of many, and it is this feeling that will show us the safest paths to a fairer and more humane society.

One day, the most authentic dreams of all human beings will join many of the other dreamers, who are already gone, releasing a current of energy so strong and so intense that it will be able to transform our planet into a place where everyone can find happiness. What I wish for everyone is a world where we can share progress and not misery.

However, for this to happen, we need people with a different profile, people who do not conform to bad things, people who are not intimidated by the crisis and difficulties, people who use creativity, understanding, humility, perseverance, motivation, and have a leadership spirit.

It is through these steps that the key to this new world is, and you are not only a mere helpless spectator in the face of all these transformations, on the contrary, you can also be one of the main characters of this wonderful play to be staged called existence.

Learn more about our work:

This material is a transcript of a motivational video with the same name, and which, although it was produced more than a decade ago, remains current and futuristic. If you want to know a little more about the subject, we recommend the full message available on our YouTube channel.

In addition, we invite all those who were touched by this reading and managed to expand their natural and especially supernatural vision, to experience a real Disruptive experience in our other titles: "The Four Types of Transformative Intelligence: Intelligences Applied to Christian Transformation in the Digital Age" and "Cryptocurrencies – The Money of the Future." Both books can have their e-book version downloaded from the author's website:

www.marcuslisboa.com.br

Author Contact:

Marcus Lisboa

Email: mvla2015@gmail.com / inepp@inepp.org.br /

eco.finances@principautedeseborga.com

Twiter: @Marcus_Lisboa38 - @interesseP

Parler: @MarcusLisboa   - @InteressePublico

Instagram: @marcusvlisboa - @doutorblockchain -

@interessepublicoBrasil

https://conservativecore.net/MarcusLisboa

Facebook: https://www.facebook.com/marcusvlisboa/

Linkedin: https://www.linkedin.com/in/bitsblockchain/

Site: www.marcuslisboa.com.br

www.inepp.org.br

www.popblockchain.com

www.cryptotech.com.br

www.ingramcontent.com/pod-product-compliance
Lightning Source LLC
LaVergne TN
LVHW021007200726

843506LV00012B/2203